SWEDISH LAGOM

INTRODUCTION TO THE SWEDISH LAGOM LIFESTYLE AND HOW TO DO IT YOURSELF

OSCAR NIELSEN

TABLE OF CONTENTS

CHAPTER 1:

Where Does Lagom Come From?

According to one best-selling author, Linnea Dunne, Lagom is the reason why the people of Sweden rank high internationally when it comes to productivity and happiness. But where does the word Lagom come from?

It's a national core value that can make people happier and more productive. And that is probably enough for some to try it.

We know that Lagom is definitely a Swedish word. If we consult our lexicons, a standard literal translation from Swedish to English will use the following words to define the word Lagom:

- Just right
- Adequate
- Sufficient
- Enough

Of course that is a standard textbook definition. Those words give us hints as to the other nuances that are related to it. Because of the implications of such terms we can say that maybe that is the reason why a lot of times the word Lagom is translated as:

- Suitable
- In balance
- In moderation

In other words, simply put, when we say Lagom we are referring to something that is just the right amount. It will carry that peculiar connotation of appropriateness. However, do take note that it does not demand perfection.

You don't have to be perfect to be Lagom. Flawlessness isn't part of the gradations of its meaning. What you're looking for actually is a balance but you don't have to be perfectly balanced to be truly Lagom.

THE LAW OF JANTE

"Lagom är bäst" as the old proverb in Sweden goes. It literally translates to "The right amount is best." What does that have to do with anything?

Imagine living in a place where the environment is both harsh and lovely. Now, it will be very difficult to picture that in one's mind. But that is the case for many Swede natives. They lived in a place where the climate is harsh during the winter.

The land is unforgiving when the snows have reached their borders. Yet when the snows are gone everything turns idyllic and almost near paradisiacal. These are the stark contrasts that the original Vikings had to deal with.

And when push comes to shove they had no one else to turn to than their family and friends. And that is why we have that old proverb: the right amount is best.

They had to share and share alike. When it came to food and drink everyone in the family should practice moderation. Everything that was consumable had to be divided equally among all present.

The right amount is best because it is for the best of everyone around you. In the end it is you who benefits from this practice. That is also perhaps why another proverb comes to mind – *There is virtue in moderation.*

And this background serves as a nice cushion for the Law of Jante. This is a code of conduct amongst the Nordic people. We learn of it from an ancient author by the name of Aksel Sandemose who is of Danish and Norwegian descent.

In his story, A Fugitive Crosses His Tracks, he tells of a small town called Jante. It was the typical town in his time—a small town where everyone knew everybody. The emphasis in the rules of Jante is to put emphasis on the benefit of the collective rather than the pursuit of individual achievement or ambition.

Remember the setup earlier? People lived in their time in a world where the lone wolf died and the pack stayed alive proverbially speaking. We can say that that is probably the reason for the paradigm being cast by Lagom as a principle of living.

So, what are the rules of Jante? There are ten of them, and here they are:

1. Do not think that you are as good as we are
2. Never think that you are smarter than we are
3. Don't think of yourself as something special
4. You are not more important than we are
5. Don't think that you know more than what we know
6. Don't imagine yourself to be better than we are
7. Don't think that anyone cares about you
8. Do not laugh at us
9. Don't think that you are good at anything
10. You can't teach us anything

THE 11TH RULE

Now, to the 20th-century mind it would seem that these ideals are clashing with other core principles like the individual pursuit of happiness, identity, achievement, and personal greatness.

No, that is not what the ten rules are trying to point out. Notice that all ten rules contrast "you" and "us." It's not that there will never come another Einstein that will teach the world new things.

Someone like that will always be appreciated by everyone who practices Lagom. Note also that there is an 11th rule, which states:

11. "Perhaps you don't think we know a few things about you?"

One educator explained that the Law of Jante is more of a social code that is aimed at encouraging group behavior. In other words the emphasis is valuing what you can do for everyone.

This principle, the Law of Jante as well as Lagom, also stresses being mindful of what you say and do since such things can impact others as well. That resonates with sayings like "no man is an island" and others along that line.

This paradigm of caring for others and looking out for other people is at the heart of the Norse peoples. It is something that we all can learn from in our modern and often disconnected world.

Sure, maybe technology has brought us a new way to get connected. But at times we have lost a sense of community and maybe Lagom can help us get back to our human roots.

CHAPTER 2:

What is Lagom and How Do I Start?

In the previous chapter we have covered the definition of Lagom so we won't go over that in much detail here. However, we just need to highlight one particular key point about this Swedish lifestyle concept and that is how it also allows people to be curious and try other things.

As anthropology expert Dr. Kathleen Bryson put it, Lagom is something akin to Goldilocks. This is a concept wherein one is looking for something that isn't too little, not too much, but just right.

In that story, Goldilocks tries different types of chairs, beds, and of course porridge. The items that were tested belonged to Papa Bear, Mama Bear, and Baby Bear. She tries everything until she finally found some of the things that suited her.

LET CURIOSITY TAKE YOU BY THE HAND

Curiosity is the first step before you can apply the Lagom lifestyle. Be curious and not judgmental. Discover areas in your life where you can apply the facets of this type of living. You don't have to apply its principles to every aspect of your life.

You can do it one step at a time one part of your life at a time. Remember the simple Goldilocks principle: not too much, not too little, but just right. Let's look at several areas where we can actually apply this peculiar Nordic lifestyle choice.

YOUR STUFF

I think you can agree that in our modern society a lot of us are preoccupied with accumulating stuff—lots of stuff. Just check out how many clothes you have in your closet. How many toys does your kid have? How many shoes do you have in the house?

Now, how about your kitchen? Find out how many gizmos you have in there. Do you have more than one blender, coffee maker, knives, kitchen tools, juicers, and others? Do you really need all of that stuff?

This is one area where we all can apply Lagom. Later in a separate chapter we will go over how to declutter your home and your life.

Remember that Lagom is all about embracing sustainability as one's way of life. As it was already pointed out it entails not consuming too much. That also means you have to make choices that are ultimately environment-friendly.

You can ask yourself the following questions:

- Which part of the house do I have too much stuff?
- Which rooms in my home are overstuffed?
- Do you I have two or three things that actually serve the same function?
- Do I have a lot of single-use items that I just throw away later?
- Do I have hand me downs or do I give away hand me downs?

TV TIME

It doesn't matter if you watch your videos on TV or you go by way of Netflix, YouTube, or some other online streaming media. According to a report from the American Academy of Pediatrics, children nowadays spend an average of 7 hours a day watching videos and other media.

Now imagine how much time grownups spend in front of a screen, any size of screens whether it's a full-size theater or your phone. According to one CNN report, adults spend an average of 10 hours each day. That means we older folks aren't really doing any better compared to our kids.

7 hours and 10 hours—that's the average viewing time. That's a lot of time to be glued onto a screen.

AT WORK

Now, a lot of people might argue that they just have to work. This is a subjective aspect of our lives and we should be left to evaluate it on our own. Nevertheless, you should still evaluate it. You should decide if you are working too little or too much.

ME TIME AND FAMILY TIME

In our hectic schedules I think everyone can agree (or at least almost everyone) can say that people aren't having enough me time and family time. Check your schedule and evaluate each item on your to-do list.

Find ways to reduce the time you spend for others to make time for yourself. You should also make more time for your family. You should also take into account how much time you spend indoors and outdoors. How much time do you sit around? Compare that to the time you spend moving.

SLEEP

Are you sleeping enough or do you hardly sleep at all? Are your thoughts and concerns so overwhelming that they keep you awake at night?

There are plenty of other areas that you need to examine and we'll go over them in this book in the chapters that follow.

CHAPTER 3:

Adopting the Lagom Mindset

In the previous chapter we talked about different ways how you can start living a Lagom lifestyle. If there is one thing about this kind of lifestyle that is truly inspiring and something that you should pick up on it is this: it is not about making things work less or work more.

What this kind of paradigm is teaching us is that we should balance in all things and make things work better.

Do we get rid of beautiful furniture because they are less functional? Of course not—what we need to do is to add beauty to functionality finally getting the necessary balance between these two aspects.

Why? It is because both beauty and functionality are important.

DIET, DIET, DIET

A lagom lifestyle is big on caring for oneself. You will begin to be more self-conscious. That means you should acknowledge where you are at right now and do more to correct things so that you will live a healthy lifestyle.

A lagom lifestyle entails maintaining a balanced diet. That means you will make a healthy choice to live healthy and to eat healthy. Does that mean you will no longer try different cuisines?

NO IT DOES NOT.

Remember the Goldilocks analogy. Let curiosity drive you forward. You should try different things, but above all else practice moderation. It shouldn't come as a surprise that the people in Sweden do not abstain from the simple pleasures of life like big servings of chocolate cake or maybe a large glass of wine.

Practicing lagom allows you to treat yourself and enjoy life's pleasures. However, do not binge. Eat, drink, enjoy things but you should know when you have had enough; and when you do, then stop.

CONTROL—IT'S ALL ABOUT SELF-CONTROL.

And that is one way how you can live a healthy and happy life.

PRACTICING KINDNESS

Another important facet of a lagom mindset is the practice of kindness. That entails being kind to yourself first and then being kind to others as well. We all make mistakes and we learn to forgive by first forgiving ourselves.

This inner kindness to oneself can then translate to being kind to other people as well. Embracing a lagom mindset will mean that you will take care of yourself because if you do then you will be empowered to take care of others.

It should be obvious that you can't help other people if you can't help yourself. You need to be standing on higher ground before you can pull other people up. The sense of community in a lagom mindset is strong because the individual is better able to care for itself.

But that doesn't mean you will not practice the principle of sacrifice. Of course when you come to a point when you want to put the needs of others like your friends and family above yours then you will do it. It is part of lagom too—in fact it is a huge part of that mindset.

However, do take note that before you can sacrifice anything you must be fit enough to provide that necessary sacrifice. And that is the cycle of it all—one thing leads to the other.

This is also why lagom is a very powerful concept in the workplace. Imagine a company where the culture is that there is no need for cutthroat competition for the next promotion at the end of the quarter. Imagine everyone from the rank and file to the top level managers being united to move the business forward.

In that environment everyone benefits from the push that the company is getting. Because everyone does their part rowing the boat everyone gets to the shore safely and quickly. It's the perfect win/win setup.

SHOPPING FOR THE LONG TERM

They practice what is called a "capsule wardrobe" in Sweden. You may already be doing it and you just don't know, so here's how it goes.

Go through your wardrobe and find all the clothes that you haven't worn in a year. Take it off your wardrobe, wash and clean up those clothes, and then pack them so you can hand them down to someone who may benefit from it. Don't throw them away. Give them away to someone who may need them.

When you buy clothes don't just buy them because they're the latest fad. Be conscientious when you shop for clothes. Consider the quality of the item you are buying. Make sure that you are buying something that will last.

You can also practice this principle in the kitchen or with anything that you are buying. By being less of a hoarder or impulse buyer you are also helping the environment by reducing the amount of waste that you will one day throw away.

CHAPTER 4:

Lagom at Home and at Work

After adopting a lagom mindset you can now apply its principles in the home and also at work. In a way you are now investing yourself in Scandinavian culture. What we know so far is that lagom is Sweden's version of mindfulness. The big difference is that it espouses two additional principles which are moderation/balance and peculiarly collective spirit.

PRACTICING LAGOM AT HOME

Note that there is no direct translation of lagom into English. We can define it in English terms but there is no linguistic equivalent of the word lagom. Translated directly or not, we can very much practice this lifestyle at home.

Here are the things that you can do to practice lagom at home.

• Learn to Slow Down and Get Out of That Rush

We always rush, don't we? In this modern world we tend to rush as soon as we open our eyes. It is as if the world has pre-programmed our lives to go quickly by getting one thing done at a time. Sometimes rushing is part of the routine. You sometimes don't notice that you are already doing it robotically—it's almost automatic.

Sometimes we rush for six days and then we take a break only on the 7th, which is some practice that has been handed down to us from religious eras—you know the idea of a Sabbath or day of rest.

That isn't so bad. We all need at least one day to stop all work, reevaluate ourselves, calibrate our bearings, and sharpen our proverbial saws. But wouldn't it be great to have some mini "Sabbaths" each day?

Lagom is all about the principles of slow living. It doesn't mean you're going to slow down like a sloth. What it means is that you will take a little paradigm shift and then you change the way you live.

We all rush to be successful in life, which we define in a variety of terms. Some define success as getting that six-figure income while others define it as being renowned in their profession.

But what if you end up like the masses that don't reach the very top or end up shy of a few hundred dollars to get to that coveted six-figure paycheck.

Lagom's answer is that it is okay.

It's okay if you don't get fame and fortune. What lagom teaches us is that getting these things is nice but they do not define who you are. In fact, our success and failures do not define us.

What truly defines us is how we live.

Slow down and appreciate all the good things that happened along the way that led you to improve your financial or professional position. You did not end up on top but you had many small victories along the way.

You took the time to celebrate each one. You don't rush to plan your next victory. You take time to celebrate each one. You do not stress to get to work ahead of time but you take time to appreciate every new beginning that life has given you.

Slow down and take time to appreciate the flowers.

• Get In Touch With Nature

When was the last time you spent at least an hour to bask in Mother Nature's radiance? The people in Sweden have a rule which they called allemansrätten. This means everyone is free to roam where they please.

It doesn't mean that you have to go to the beach each weekend or you have to take that monstrous hike. It can be anything from a walk in the park or even taking the time to care for your lawn.

What is important is that you take the time to get in touch with nature. Get reconnected to the very thing that gives us all life and breath since the day we were born. Regaining that connection will enthuse you with a kind of refreshing renewal to energize you and help you face the difficulties that you have to endure day in and day out.

• Simplify Your Possessions

Again, another thing that you can do at home is to live a minimalistic lifestyle. We'll go over that in a separate chapter.

• Practice Fika at Home

In Sweden, Fika means to have that simple extra snack time that is spent with friends or coworkers. This Fika is usually relaxed, slow paced, and cozy. You all enjoy some coffee or maybe some pastry together and talk about anything under the sun. The vibe during Fika is relaxed and non-critical and very congenial.

Now imagine doing that at home. When was the last time that you had a chance to sit down and enjoy cake with your spouse or your kids? When was the last time you sat down and enjoyed a drink together to have a relaxed conversation? These are moments when you can reconnect and reinforce your relationship.

• Do It for the Family

Lagom is not about quitting the pursuit for individual greatness, not at all. However, what you're going to do is to change the motive from I'm doing this all for me to I'm doing this for the family.

You're working hard for that promotion because you want something better for the family. Your kids do their best at school because they're doing it for the family. Later on they will learn to be great at what they do so that they can contribute to the country and to society as a whole.

PRACTICING LAGOM IN THE WORKPLACE

We have described above five practices that can help you practice lagom at home. You can actually use the same practices at work:

- Get out of the rush cycle
- Get in touch with nature
- Simplify material possessions
- Do some Fika
- Pursue success for the community

We can translate that in the workplace like this:

1. **Quit the rush**—simplify all to-do lists by refining office procedures getting rid of unnecessary steps. Streamline the workflow and make it easy for everyone. Simplify complicated processes and empower every member of the organization so they can do their own part to the best of their ability.

2. **Get in touch with nature**—go for a green workplace. Switch to paperless offices. Allow all workers to take nature breaks. You can even bring Mother Nature's touch in the workplace by having a small garden or at least add a few potted plants sparsely all over the office building. Sometimes all you need to do is to open the windows and let the sunshine in.

3. **Simplify material possessions**—again this is all about minimalism. Do you have excess tools, equipment, and fixtures in the office? They're just taking up space and you're not going to need them anyway. Why not sell them to your employees or auction them away to the public. That way you recover part of your invested capital.

4. **Do some Fika**—managers and staff and pretty much everyone will benefit from these small conversations. It will foster trust and openness in the workplace.

5. **Pursue success for the community**—imagine how much more productive everyone will be when everyone's focus is to help make the business grow.

CHAPTER 5:

The Lagom Lifestyle

We have mentioned several times in this book that the lagom lifestyle has a huge emphasis on community spirit and collaboration. However, not everyone is fit for that kind of dynamic.

Some people are lone wolves so to speak. They do things better when they left to themselves. But that doesn't mean they can't work with others or contribute to any kind of group effort.

The question is this—can the philosophy of lagom work for them as well?

The answer is yes—they can apply this philosophy to their lives as well. So, let's say you are more of an introvert and you prefer to do things on your own. Here are a few ways you can apply lagom and create space for collaboration as well. The tips and ideas presented here can work both at home and at work.

ORGANIZE: CREATE A SYSTEM THAT ANYONE CAN EASILY PICK UP ON

Do you prefer that people do not disturb you when you're in the middle of something? Well, I guess that can happen to a lot of folks and not only to solo style workers and introverts.

You can easily create or simply adopt one of the systems that the Swedes have used. For instance, to reduce office or home clutter you can set up a box, a basket, or even a box (any container that is big enough will do) at a conspicuous space. The Swedes put this bag or basket by the stairs so that everyone just passes by it and everyone can see it right away.

This container is where you will put every bit of clutter or misplaced item that is found lying around in the office. That way when something goes missing or when something is misplaced and have been found, it will just be placed in there.

And if anyone discovers that they may have something missing they can use that as some kind of lost and found section. However, here's the thing. When that receptacle gets full that is your signal that it is time to sort things out.

Go through all of that stuff and put every item where it belongs. A small basket or a container that you can carry around will be better suited for that purpose. You can do that by yourself and if you have guests or visitors in the house you can quickly explain what that basket or box is for.

You can also apply this same principle in the office. You can put several trays on your desk or office. One tray is for requests that people want from you, another tray will be for notes that they think you should see, another tray is for stuff that other people wanted to get done that you have already finished.

You can also create this kind of organization using other items or other tools so that people can leave you alone to concentrate on your work. That way the flow you have going on while working won't be compromised. It's very hard to get back into full concentration after you have been interrupted, right?

SETTING UP THE AMBIENCE

Candles are a big thing in Sweden and it shouldn't come as a surprise that they are part of that lagom lifestyle as well. In their culture, people would rather buy a lamp or some other form of lighting than buy some kind of furniture, like maybe a dining table or something.

Some people can dig that part about candles setting up the atmosphere and ambiance of a place while others can't. Some folks won't be too keen on setting up a lot of candles in the house like the Swedes do. That is especially true if there are kids in the house. You don't want to start a fire because your kid knocked down a candle by accident.

But it's not exactly about the candles that make them such a huge thing in Sweden. What you're actually looking for is the effect of the lighting and the scent of the candles. The light effect and scent have a direct impact on a person's mood.

You can install dimmers in your house to adjust the lighting. You can set it to brighter light to keep you more alert and to help you concentrate on work. You can dim the lights to induce a more relaxed atmosphere when you need it.

You can use essential oils with electric diffusers and place them in strategic areas in the office or in your home. You can use this combination of lights and scents to improve the mood if the day turns out to be particularly stressful.

This is one practice that will be particularly useful during the cold winter months when the nights are longer. You won't get enough sunlight so you can do what you can and create artificial light to balance your mood. The scent of candles or from essential oils can help soothe your soul.

TAKE TIME FOR FIKA AND/OR BADA BASTU

We have gone over the practice of fika in a previous chapter in this book. It has particular benefits when it comes to fostering better ties with friends and colleagues.

Another practice of the Swedes that you should know about (which is also part of the lagom lifestyle) is taking frequent saunas. They call it the bada bastu. It's a refreshing practice and it is a rather welcome treat when the colder winter months come along.

The Swedes in particular can take these saunas alone or with a group. You can go to saunas and enjoy the experience on your own or you can go there with friends.

It's a great detoxifying experience since the heat flushes away all the impurities. This hot and cold experience will help improve your body's blood circulation and it also perks up your mood.

Even if you're an introvert you can still invite one or two friends to come along with you. Share the experience. It may also help you improve your social skills as well.

TV TIME WITH FRIENDS AND FAMILY

Now, here is something that American families used to have. It gradually disappeared with the advent of internet streaming video—thank you Netflix! Back in the day we used to have family TV nights where mom, dad, and the kids would gather around the TV to watch our favorite shows.

Well, you can't do that anymore since we're all glued to each of our own screens. You can bring back this timeless tradition in your family at least once a week. You don't have to stick to the program on TV.

You can grab a movie from the internet too if you want. Choose something that everyone in the family can agree on. You can then prepare a family snack while you're watching it.

You can even rent a video if you want some old school vid that brings back a lot of fond memories. If you're living alone then you can invite a friend to come over. You can even catch up with a long lost friend and invite them over for some popcorn and a classic video that you both enjoyed when you were kids.

It's not the show that is important. The important thing is that you are able to reconnect with friends and family and renew those bonds of friendship. Remember that it doesn't matter how much of a loner you are.

Human beings are social creatures and even the most loner of loners will still need a friend from time to time.

VEGAN SLASH SEMI-VEGAN DIET

Another part of lagom philosophy is that of mindful eating. You don't buy food just for the sake of eating good food. Experts say that eating beef leaves a larger carbon footprint than driving a car.

That's how much the preparation and consumption of beef impact the environment. You don't have to be completely vegan 100%. You can be part vegan or just reduce your beef intake—that means fewer burgers or steaks a week if you know what I mean.

It will also mean that you should be taking more veggies during the week. Making that dietary change will improve your health. On top of that, you will also help the environment. Now this is a way to apply lagom philosophy whether you're an introvert or not.

BARGAIN SHOPPING

The Swedes have lots of flea markets that they call "loppis." They love to buy second-hand items and they are usually sold for a fraction of the cost of brand new clothing. It's not just clothing that you can find in second-hand shops.

Sure you can find chic clothing too and they are sold very cheap. You can find a lot of items from lampshades to kitchen appliances. Just make sure to check the quality of the item before you pay for it.

There are also plenty of online stores that sell second-hand items. You can also practice lagom by carefully and thoughtfully do some smart shopping for second-hand items. In a way you are preserving the environment and practicing lagom as well.

This is again one way to practice this philosophy on your own. You can share this practice with friends and relatives turning it into a community experience if you want.

CHAPTER 6:

Lagom Minimalism

As you make small cultural shifts into a lagom lifestyle you will begin to understand that by owning a few things only you will feel healthier. You will feel some sort of release from all the clutter. It can even foster a brighter outlook in life.

Your point of view will slowly shift from that of focusing on material possessions to that of focus on things that are truly meaningful and absolutely lasting. This is no less than an appealing idea.

That is why this idea or lifestyle is gaining such a huge following. Some people call it lagom, some call it essentialism, while others call it minimalism. However, what people don't realize is that these three concepts are not synonymous.

Yes, lagom is not exactly minimalism, minimalism is not essentialism, and essentialism is not lagom. However, they do have common features, which is why people use any of these terms loosely.

All things considered, we can say that lagom and essentialism are the easier or softer versions of minimalism. Another way to put it is that lagom has its own twist (a Swedish tweak?) on what mainstream minimalism is all about. We'll go over each of these concepts in the discussion below taking note of their differences as well as their similarities.

WHAT IS MINIMALISM?

Some people think of minimalism as living on bare bones belongings. You can even imagine empty rooms with very minimal furnishings and a family having only a few possessions.

Those maybe stark images that people imagine but minimalists aren't really like that. The practice actually varies from one person to the next. Of course there are extreme minimalists who do live on bare bones belongings but they aren't the rule when it comes to this philosophy.

Most people focus on the belongings that a person owns when they talk about minimalism. But it isn't really all about owning less and being happy with it. It does apply that, yes, but it is more than that.

Minimalism's focus is actually on the core values of the individual. The actual focus is on what one really wants out of this life. By owning fewer things one gets away from the distractions of wanting to own more.

The lifestyle focus of modern minimalism is only one way to practice this philosophy. A minimalist values and focuses on intentionality. That is why they only own that which is necessary. They intentionally focus only on the things that they actually need so that they can focus on the truly valuable things in life.

HOW DOES THAT DIFFER FROM ESSENTIALISM?

On the surface essentialism may seem to be just like minimalism. Well, it also zeroes in on the essentials of life. The concept of essentialism was introduced by best-selling author Greg McKeown.

His writings were mainly targeted towards businesses and the corporate life but the ideas that he presented can greatly be applied to personal living as well. Yes, both essentialism and minimalism teach that one should live with less material things.

But the difference that makes essentialism quite different is in the fact that it emphasizes owning less but getting better things. In simple terms what essentialism focuses on is quality over quantity.

It's not just in the owning of the bare essentials that are necessary here. If you are an essentialist you will look for the best quality in everything that you will own and possess.

Note that essentialism isn't only about possessions. Yes you strip down your wardrobe in this practice as well just as you would in minimalism and lagom. But you also strip away unnecessary time commitments, unnecessary things that drain your mental focus, unnecessary emotional burdens, and other non-material facets in your life. If something does not improve the quality of your life you will toss it out.

The essentialist in you will value quality—that is the emphasis. You will also focus on getting less but you do it in lieu of getting something better.

LAGOM VERSION OF MINIMALISM

In the Swedish version of minimalism, you don't necessarily have to go down to bare-bones levels. You will own less because you only want what is enough for you. You will emphasize simplicity in the things that you own and do.

However, you will also add a touch of coziness and comfort in your lifestyle. And that is not entirely bare bones as it were. In practice, you will also avoid overworking since that will put less emphasis on the other aspects of your life.

A lagomist will practice minimalism to the point where he or she has attained balance in life. You will practice owning less but putting emphasis on not having too much or too little. What you are actually aiming for is getting the things that are just right.

PRACTICING LAGOM MINIMALISM IN THE HOME

Now, practicing lagom minimalism can't be done all in one day. Well, that will depend on how much clutter you need to get rid of. It will entail a lot of sacrifices and you will feel like you're parting with some of the things that you are most emotionally attached to.

However, by taking the time and effort to practice lagom in the home you will be able to find the most precious things in your life and focus on those things first. Note that you will undergo the deepest house cleaning you will ever do in your life.

So, clear your schedule and allot at least 1 to 3 hours a day for 7 days.

Day 1—Closets

Start day 1 during the weekdays. You should allot day 6 and day 7 for the weekends. Trust me; you're going to need a lot of time during those last two days.

Day 1 decluttering should be easy enough. Your closets are the easiest to start with which is why most people begin with that.

Prepare three big boxes (or any size that will be big enough for you). One box should be labeled as the donate box, the second one will be labeled as the consignment box, and the last one is the throw-away box.

Now, here is the rule that we have talked about earlier in this book. There is actually only just one rule but if you want to add a few more additional rules for the sake of functionality (i.e. clothes that you may use in a future time) then you can add them.

Here is the rule again: if a piece of clothing or any clothing article hasn't been used or worn in a year then it should be removed from your closet. Of course there are exceptions, which are the additional rules that we have mentioned earlier.

If you have a special suit or dress or maybe a costume that you may wear in the future (like a Spiderman costume or a tuxedo or maybe a gown that you reserve for special occasions) then they don't have to get taken down.

Now, here's another important rule—if it doesn't fit you anymore then it definitely has to go away. Go through all the stuff in your closet and spare no drawers. Everything should be examined and evaluated.

You will end up with four groups of clothing articles:

1. Clothes that fit you, clothes that you will continue to wear this year, special clothing that you may use in the future – these will stay in your closet.

2. Clothes that still fit and still look dazzlingly good but you no longer use or wear – these clothes will go into consignment, something that you can sell somewhere or to a garage sale that you will want to do in the coming days.

3. Clothes that are in good shape but you don't want to sell (stuff that you think someone like a friend might want) – these will go to the donate box; always think of someone or maybe a charity to whom you will want to donate these clothes.

4. The rest, which includes the ones that don't fit you anymore or are just not wearable, will go into the box for throwing away.

Organize your closet after sorting. Bring the donations box to a charity or to the person you intend to give it away to. The ones for consignment should be taken to a thrift store or some place that will take them and then the ones for throwing away should be thrown away.

Do this immediately. Do not delay.

Day 2—Bathroom

The bathroom should be either the easiest place to organize or the second easiest. Well, there should be a lot less stuff in the bathroom to organize. In fact, you can switch, do the bathroom on day 1 and the closet on day 2.

But it's all up to you. I just put the closet on day one since it will have a lot of emotional baggage—trust me it will. Those clothes will trigger a lot of emotions. It's best that you get rid of the emotional stuff first so that the rest of the process will be a lot easier.

Reorganizing your bathroom will be a lot easier since most of the stuff you'll find here can only be placed into two categories—for use and for throwing away. You will hardly find anything that you can recycle in the bathroom.

Here are my tips to de-clutter your bathroom:

• Medicine Cabinet

This should be the easiest area in the bathroom to organize. It will contain all your meds and other stuff. Check the label of each item and then throw away the ones that are already expired.

• Beach Stuff

Sunscreens, tanning lotions, facial masks, and skin care products come next. Again, check the expiration and throw away the ones that are expired.

• Beauty Items

Hair care products, makeup, and other related items are next in line. Check your hair spray, shampoo, conditioners, facial scrubs, and other beauty products. Sort them out.

• Toilet Paper

If you find extra or unused toilet paper, then store them. Preferably in a see-through cabinet where they are easy to reach or you can put them in an area where they can be easily found.

• Linens

If you have a linen closet then it's time to sort out the items in there. Anything that is dingy or won't be used anymore should be thrown away.

• Stuff on the Sink

The stuff on the sink has to go—it's either that or put them elsewhere. There should only be a minimal amount of things on the sink counter. It should only contain the stuff that you use everyday nothing more.

Makeup and hair products should go in a separate cabinet or drawer. Another option is to put all your usable hair products in one bin and the makeup in a separate container.

Day 3—Kitchen

The kitchen should be another easy spot to de-clutter. A lot of the stuff that you need to check would be hidden away inside cabinets. You might be surprised to find how creative you were when trying to fit everything in such small spaces.

At other times the clutter that you need to sort out will just be hidden in plain sight. Yes, they will be on your countertops. I suggest that you work with the cabinets first so that you can create more room in there for the stuff that you will really need to use.

Remember, the same rules apply—if something looks like you have never used it in a year then you should toss it out. If something will definitely never be used this year, then it has to go away as well. If something could be used sometime in the future (like a special Asian noodle maker for instance) that will be used in your anniversary or some other special occasion then store it.

Here are a few organization tips that might help:

• Plastic containers and Tupperware

Oh I had a lot of this at home. It was really a surprise to me when I opened up my cabinets. I couldn't believe how much Tupperware I had lying around the house!

Keep the containers that still have matching tops and bottoms. You won't believe how many extras these things have so you can either choose to throw away or give away the extras. Put these in a box.

Stained containers have to go (they should go into recycling) unless you can find a way to re-purpose them like turn them into pots for plants or something. The ones you intend to repurpose should be placed in a separate container while those you are throwing away for recycling can go into a garbage bag.

• Knives and other Utensils

Utensils that you still use and will be using until next year should go to a separate container. Put the ones that you won't be using anymore in a box that will be for consignment. If you find ones that you think can be recycled then put them in a separate box.

You should decide which knives you're going to be using in the coming months. Place the knives and other cutlery that you are no longer going to use in a separate box. Consider selling them or recycling them. Go through the other utensils and kitchen appliances and sort them out in this manner as well.

Pick the pots and pans that you will be using. There will usually some that you no longer use. Put them in a separate box and decide whether you will give them away or throw them away.

Make sure to separate the pots from the pans. The pots can be stacked and you can store the tops separately. That should help to get things organized.

Place the Tupperware, pots, pans, kitchen tools, countertop appliances, and other stuff in their separate shelves. The ones that have to go should be disposed of as soon as possible. Do this today or first thing in the morning.

Keep only as few countertop items as possible.

Day 4—Books, Toys, and All the Stuff in the Living Room

On day 3 go over the stuff in your living room including all the toys, books, magazines, and other things that can be found there. Grab a basket (you can order cheap ones on Amazon) or repurpose an old container or box and put that by the staircase or in any area corridor where everyone usually passes by.

That box or container/basket is where you will put all the misplaced or otherwise lost items. When the box gets filled, place the items in the designated spot where they should be. Remember to throw away toys and any stuff that you or your kids no longer use.

Day 5—Bedroom

There should never be anything under your bed—nothing. They will just gather dust there. Dresser tops and cabinet tops should also be inspected, de-cluttered, and cleaned. Follow the same rules as before when sorting things out.

Place a laundry basket in a corner that is hidden from view. That's where all the laundry goes.

Day 6—Basement and Attic

Basement and/or attic day should be done on the weekend—maybe on a Saturday. You will spend more time here than on the other days. You should get some help when you sort things out on day 6.

Follow the same rules as before. Tents, fishing gear, and other equipment will have to be stored separately. The same thing is true for holiday decorations and other specialty items.

Day 7—Garage

Again, you might want to get some help when organizing your garage. You will follow the same rules as before but you will need a few organizers to get the garage fixed up.

I recommend that you install shelves and peg boards up on the walls to help get things organized. Yard tools can be hung on the boards and the tools that don't fit in your toolbox should go into the shelves.

CHAPTER 7:

How Lagom Differs With the Seasons

In this chapter we will go over how lagom is applied to how we eat. Well, specifically how Nordic recipes come into the picture. Lagom also gives you no extremes way of eating.

That means your diet should never be too restrictive. You should never deprive yourself of good food. However, just as we have explained in earlier sections of this book, your diet shouldn't be all about binge eating as well. Yes, it's back to Goldilocks tasting all the porridge on sight kind of thing.

A lagom diet or should we say Nordic or Swedish diet to be exact is one that mixes vegetables, fish, whole grains, and a few helpings of poultry as needed. There will also be plenty of fika during the mid-day. Don't worry; you won't run out of sweet treats with this diet.

Let's go over several recipes that are served with the changing seasons.

Spring Time Recipes

CABBAGE SLAW RECIPE

This is a classic for springtime. It is also a great side dish for any main course. You can even serve this green slaw with pizza to complement the meaty and cheese filled flavor.

Ingredients:

- White cabbage (1 pound)
- Red onion (1 small piece, sliced finely)
- Bell pepper (1 piece, sliced)
- Cold-pressed olive oil (3 Tbsp)
- White wine vinegar (1 Tbsp)
- Dried oregano (1/2 tsp)
- Red pepper flakes (just a pinch)
- Poppy seeds (1 tsp)
- Sunflower seeds (1 tsp)

Procedure:

Shred cabbage into fine pieces. You can use a food processor with a slicing attachment. Sprinkle some sea salt on cabbage and let it sit for half an hour. Drain water from cabbage and place in a large bowl.

Add onion and red pepper. Whisk together olive oil, vinegar, chili flakes, oregano, and black pepper in a separate bowl. This serves as the dressing.

Pour dressing mixture onto sliced cabbage. Give it a good toss. Grab some pizza, sausage, or any main course and enjoy it with this cabbage slaw.

CHERRY JAM

This is a great jam for dessert. You can grab a spoonful of this thing if you have a sweet tooth. You can also use it on sandwiches or even breakfast rolls.

Ingredients:

- Fresh cherries (400 g, stoned)
- Lemon juice (½ lemon)
- Vanilla pod (1 piece, halved lengthwise)
- Golden caster sugar (150 g)

Procedure:

Place a large enough saucer in the freezer. You will use this later to cool off the jam once it is cooked. Mix together the vanilla pod, lemon juice, and the cherries. Add 1 tbsp. of sugar. Mix well.

Simmer until the sugar is completely dissolved. Add one more tablespoon of sugar and repeat the process. Keep adding a tablespoonful of sugar to the mixture until all your sugar has been added.

Keep simmering until the mixture is jammy. Take the saucer out of the freezer and place the jam in it. Leave it there to cool. You can tell if it is completely cooled when you can push one finger through the cherry jam.

Once cooled pour contents into a storage jar. Use as necessary.

Summer Time Recipes

SPRING NETTLE SOUP

This nice soup adds a nice touch of green to a hot summer. It's a great way to either start your day in case you want to start light or for a companion to an evening meal. It is said that the Swedes flock to the forests on hot summer days to pick nettles and other ingredients for soups like this. Of course you can buy yours from the store rather than picking them fresh off the forest.

Ingredients:

- Nettle shoots (8 cups)
- Butter (3 tbsp.)
- Salt (1 tsp.)
- Chopped chives (1/2 cup)
- Chicken bouillon (1 cube)
- Vegetable bouillon (1 cube)
- Crème fraîche (1/2 cup)
- Dried thyme (1 tsp)
- Hard boiled eggs (4 pieces)
- White pepper (just a pinch)
- Cornflour (1 tsp.)
- Water (4 1/2 cups)

Procedure:

Rinse nettles (be careful they can sting). Remove all traces of dirt. Boil nettles in a pot in high heat. Add a teaspoon of water once the water starts to boil. After adding the salt, reduce to medium heat and cook the nettles for 5 minutes.

Strain off the nettles and throw away the water. Allow the nettles to cool for a few minutes and then chop them into fine pieces.

Melt butter in a pot over medium heat. Add chives and cook them for a couple of minutes. Add the bouillon cubes until they are completely dissolved in the butter mixture.

Add nettles, mix them, and then add 3.5 cups of water. Add white pepper to taste. Dissolve corn flour in half a cup of water and then stir it into the soup mixture. Serve with bread or boiled eggs. This recipe makes 4 servings.

TOSCAKAKA

This is an almond caramel cake recipe. The name translates to tosca cake and it is a classic Swedish recipe. It is very nutty and makes 8 servings.

Ingredients:

- Unsalted butter (1 cup)
- Caster sugar (¾ cup)
- Large eggs (4 pieces)
- All-purpose flour (½ cup)
- Baking powder (1 tsp)
- Salt (1/4 tsp)
- Ground almonds (1 cup)

For the toppings

- Flaked almonds (1 cup, sliced)
- Unsalted butter (½ cup)
- Light brown sugar (1/2 cup)
- Sea salt (just a pinch)
- Milk (3 tbsp)

Procedure:

Preheat oven to 360°F. Grease an 8-inch cake tin. Line it with some parchment paper. Beat the butter using an electric mixer until it becomes light and creamy. Add sugar and keep beating until the mixture becomes fluffy (this will take about 5 minutes or more after adding sugar). Add eggs until everything is mixed well.

Sift baking powder and flour. Mix together and then add ground almonds plus salt. Add this to the butter mixture and then fold your batter. Pour the batter in your prepared tin. Level it all out. Place it in the oven to bake.

For the topping:

Place all topping ingredients in a pan and mix them well. Cook over medium heat until the sugar has completely melted and caramelized. This will take about 5 minutes. Take it out of the heat when done.

Take the cake out when done. Top it with the topping mixture. Place the topped cake back inside the oven and bake for 10 more minutes. Take the cake out and let it cool. Serve and enjoy with some coffee.

Autumn Recipes

TJÄLKNÖL

Tjälknöl is a reindeer meat recipe and it reveals how the Swedes prepare large portions of meat for feasts and other occasions.

Ingredients:

- Boneless reindeer meat (2 lbs)
- Water (4 cups)
- Salt (1 cup)
- Sugar (2 tbsp)
- Bay leaf (1 piece)
- Crushed black pepper (1 tsp)
- Juniper berries (crushed, 2 tbsp)

Procedure:

Preheat oven to 170°F. Place reindeer meat on a rack and bake it at that temperature. Bake for three hours. You know that it is done when you stick a meat thermometer and it reads 150°F.

When the meat is cooked take it out of the oven. Boil the rest of the ingredients in a saucepan for 2 minutes. This will serve as the marinade. Marinade the reindeer meat in a container that is large enough. Marinade it for 5 hours.

Take the meat out and cut it into thin slices. Serve with potatoes or soup and of course some wine.

VÄSTERBOTTEN CHEESE PIE

This cheese pie is best served hot and it's great for the cooler months.

Ingredients:

For the pie pastry:

- Butter (125 g)
- Wheat flour (300 ml)
- Water (1 tbsp)

For the filling:

- Grated Västerbottensost (300 g)
- Medium size eggs (3 pieces)
- Whipped cream (200 ml)
- Black pepper (1 pinch)

Procedure:

Preheat oven to 437°F. Using a food processor mix flour and butter until the texture becomes crumbly. Add water and continue mixing until the dough becomes smooth. Press into the pie dish. Prick the pie shell and put into the oven. Bake for 10 minutes. Take it out of the oven.

Whisk cream and eggs together. Add cheese and then season with salt and pepper. Pour this filling into shell — Bake for 20 minutes. Let cool for a few minutes or you can also serve it hot.

Winter Recipes

SWEDISH CRISP PANCAKES

Swedish pancakes are thin and crisp unlike the pancakes that we are used to. You can think of them as crepes with a lot of sweet goodness to them.

Ingredients:

- Eggs (3, large)
- Milk (2 cups)
- Unbleached all-purpose flour (1 cup)
- Melted butter (unsalted, 6 tablespoons)
- Granulated sugar (1 tbsp)
- Kosher salt (1/2 tsp)
- Vanilla extract (1/2 tsp)
- Garnish (fruit of your choice, confectioner's sugar, jam, etc.)

Procedure:

In a food processor, combine eggs and milk until smooth. Add flour and combine until smooth. Add butter, milk, salt, vanilla, and sugar. Mix all ingredients until smooth.

Heat Swedish pancake pan using medium heat. Place 1 tbsp. of batter and cook until the edges have turned golden brown (takes 3 minutes on average). Flip over and cook the other side. You can use a non-stick pan alternatively but butter it up first.

Add garnish and serve.

ÄRTSOPPA

This is a Swedish classic split-pea soup. It's a great dish for cold Thursdays and this goes well with the pancakes above.

Ingredients:

- Dried yellow peas (or green ones if you can't find yellow peas, 1 pound)
- Water (8 cups)
- Onions (finely chopped, 2 cups)
- Whole onion studded with 2 cloves
- Chopped carrot (1/2 cup)
- 3 ham hocks
- Dried thyme (1 teaspoon)
- Ground ginger (1 teaspoon)
- Salt (1 teaspoon)
- Pepper (1/8 teaspoon)
- Grainy brown mustard (1 teaspoon)

Procedure:

Rinse dried peas and pick through them. You only need the ones that are whole. Soak them in water over night until they grow to 2 inches thick.

Get 6 cups water and put that into a pot. Drain peas and add them in. Add onions, carrots, ham hocks, and then boil them.

Skim off any foam. Simmer down to low heat and cook for 90 minutes. Check from time to time and remove any pea skin that floats.

Take 2 cups of the soup and puree them blender. Return the pureed soup into the pot. Simmer for 30 more minutes. Remove meat and chop it up and then put it back into soup. Season with salt, pepper, thyme, and ginger simmer for 15 minutes.

Serve with pancakes or bread. Add mustard as desired.

CHAPTER 8 :

My Favorite Lagom Drinks

We have gone over some of the best lagom food in the previous chapter. I particularly love the desserts though. In the next chapter we'll go over 20 of the best lagom foods that you can find from the Swedish cuisine.

In this chapter I would like to share my two favorite lagom drinks.

GLØGG

This is a great drink for the cold winter months. You can also serve it for Christmas dinner.

Ingredients:
- Dry red wine (3 cups, filled ¼ of the way)
- Spiced rum (1 cup)
- Honey (1 cup)
- Cardamom pods (1 tablespoon)
- Allspice berries (1 tablespoon)
- Whole cloves (2 teaspoons)
- Orange juice (1/2 cup)
- Orange peel
- 2 cinnamon sticks (4 inches each)
- Dried ginger (1-inch piece)

Instructions:

Mix all the ingredients in a saucepan cooking over medium heat. Once the mixture starts to boil simmer it for 1 hour over low heat.

Serve. Garnish with orange slices.

ISBJÖRN COCKTAIL

The name of this vodka-based cocktail means "polar bear." It is sweet and a great welcoming addition to any party you may be hosting.

Ingredients:

- Ice cubes
- Vodka (2 ounces)
- Blue curacao (1 ounce)
- Lemonade/Sprite (6 ounces)

Procedure:

Fill a glass (about 300 ml or so) with ice cubes. Add Vodka, then caracao, and then top with lemonade. Stir and serve. This makes one glass.

CHAPTER 9:

20 Healthy Lagom Foods for the Happiest Balanced Day Ever

Food that is truly lagom isn't restrictive—and that is the surprising thing about this lifestyle philosophy. There isn't any shortage in flavor and in servings but it is the principle of eating in moderation that keeps the Swedes in tip-top shape.

That makes eating the lagom way a sure treat especially for those who want to do some serious lifestyle change and lose weight at the same time. Here are my favorite lagom foods and I hope that they will be yours too.

1. KÖTTBULLAR

This is a kind of Swedish meatballs and it is considered as their quintessential dish. This is probably the first dish to come to mind for a lot of people who have been to Sweden. The meat is usually a combination of beef and pork but it can be made of other types of meat as well.

The sauce is very flavorful and it is laced with pickled cucumbers and lingonberries. The Swedes really love their berries.

2. KANELBULLE

This spiced cinnamon bun is a type of staple in the country. I swear every café and every bakery has one of these. All you have to do is follow the scent. It is made from their very own wheat bread called vetebröd. Sometimes it is cinnamon flavored but it times it can also be vanilla or saffron flavored. You can say that this is the preferred pastry for fika.

3. SURSTRÖMMING

This is a kind of pickled herring. It has a rather sweet taste to it which complements the fresh taste of the herring. It is usually a part of the entrée and it is served either with rye bread or some boiled potatoes.

4. FILMJÖLK

This is a hot frothy drink that has a rather yogurt taste to it. Some compare it to buttermilk while others identify the flavor as akin to soured milk. Whatever it is, this drink is one that is full of healthy bacteria that will give your gut a healthy boost. It's great with cakes, bread, or even cereal.

5. REINDEER PATÉ

This pate is of course made from reindeer meat. It is very flavorful and surprisingly creamy. It's great on crackers and you can also spread it on bread.

6. OAT MILK LATTE

This is a tasty treat for anyone who is lactose intolerant or gluten intolerant. It is milk made from oats. It has a nutty taste and slightly sweet.

7. SVENSKA FISKSOPPA

This is a popular Swedish fish soup. There's plenty of fish in Sweden so it shouldn't come as a surprise that they have lots of seafood recipes. They usually make it from fresh fish and it will be served seasoned to perfection.

8. TOAST SKAGEN

Want more seafood? Try this dish—it's a prawn cocktail. It is flavored using lemon, dill, and mayonnaise. It is served with sautéed bread that has been cooked to a nice crisp texture. Skagen is actually the name of a fishing port that is located in the northern regions of Denmark. I guess that's where this dish originated from.

9. GRAVADLAX

 More fish dishes coming up! This is actually a cured salmon salad. It is cured using a mixture of salt, sugar, and dill. It is much sweeter than the salmon you will find back home and it is a great pair with potatoes.

10. FORAGED BERRIES

Yes Swedes love foraging. In fact, some consider it to be a rite of passage for them. They don't just pick berries in the wild. They are skilled at finding herbs, mushrooms, and other food growing in the wild. You get pure unadulterated flavor right from Mother Nature herself.

11. VARMRÖKT LAX

This is a smoked salmon. The Swedish twist is in using Alderwood. Note that their salmon is only lightly smoked but the flavor is kept intact.

12. Different Ways to Enjoy Herring

The North Atlantic Ocean and the Baltic Sea is full of herring and that is why it is almost a staple in Sweden. They actually have a lot of different herring recipes. My favorites are soused herring, which is known locally as Matjes. Another favorite is Strömming, which is herring that is breaded and fried.

13. VÄSTERBOTTEN

The majority of the cheeses you'll find sold in Sweden are imported. But there is one particular cheese that is really made there. It's called Västerbotten. This is cow's milk that has been aged for at least 1 full year. It has a strong flavor and it has these crystalized bits in it.

14. GODIS

There is a tradition in Sweden called lördagsgodis, which roughly translates to "Saturday sweets." Godis of course means sweets. If you go to the grocery stores where they will usually have a pick and mix of sweets from salty liquorice to chocolate covered caramels. So, you still think that lagom diet is restrictive?

15. HAMBURGARE

The first time I saw Swedish hamburgers I said to myself "no way." They do know how to make really darn good burgers. Again there is no particular kind of burger I would recommend but anything will be great as long as you only eat burgers in moderation.

16. HUSMANSKOST

Husmanskost isn't really a dish but it is more of a style of cooking—home cooked meals, well that's the closest translation I can give you. Most of the time this would mean meatballs but it can be anything since it is the "home owner's choice" (the literal translation of the word "husmanskost").

17. SWEDISH BREAD

I don't know if there is really such a thing as "Swedish bread" since there is plenty of types of bread in Sweden. This is a flatbread that is topped with nuts and seeds.

18. PRINSESSTÅRTA

This dish was created back in 1920 by a local chef named Jenny Åkerström. She was teaching Swedish princesses how to cook and dedicated this particular cake recipe to them. It's a sponge cake with several layers and it is dome-shaped. It is covered in marzipan on the exterior. This is Sweden's cake of choice apparently for celebrations and such.

19. RÄKSMÖRGÅS

This is a shrimp sandwich. Sometimes it is served as a salad with bread on the side or as a sandwich. The shrimp is usually topped with mayo, eggs, and lemon. A bit of fair warning, this is a heavy meal. All that protein will be tasty and quite tempting.

20. NYPONSOPPA

This is rosehip soup. Rosehips are usually served as tea but the Swedes make them into soup by boiling them in sugar and water. The soup is then thickened using potato flour. Its aroma is a bit flowery, which is weird but gets past that and you will taste soup that can be served either hot or cold.

CHAPTER 10:

15 Day Lagom Challenge

Now, here's the big challenge. Now that you know all about the lagom lifestyle, you should apply it within the month for 15 days. Mark your calendar when you should begin and when the challenge will end. After these 15 days are done try to evaluate the effects of lagom in your life.

Here's your schedule:

Day 1

Wake up each morning 30 minutes earlier. Begin the day with stretches and a cup of coffee. If you don't like coffee you can have tea or your favorite morning drink. Do this for the next 15 days. Start your day in a relaxed mood each day for 15 days.

Day 2

De-clutter your closet. Prepare 1 lagom meal. Remember to wake up early and exercise/stretch.

Day 3

Wake up early and stretch/exercise. You should be doing this each morning.

Don't rush your coffee breaks. Have fika with friends and coworkers. If you're at home have fika with your family members or if you're alone then have a relaxing fika break by yourself.

Day 4

De-clutter your bathroom (follow instructions in chapter 6). Have 2 lagom meals.

Day 5

De-clutter your kitchen. Have 2 lagom meals today. Take an afternoon walk in the park. 2 meals should be lagom from this time forward. Remember to inspect your fridge and don't let anything go to waste.

Day 6

Practice the art of listening with intent. Don't rush to talk. Stay relaxed whatever the type of conversation you're having. Listen intently and don't just wait for your chance to butt in and say your piece.

Fix up your yard even for a little bit.

All your meals for the day should be lagom starting today.

Day 7

De-clutter your living room. Take frequent breaks in between.

Day 8

Share your lagom experience with a friend. Enjoy fika together as a nice introduction.

Day 9

De-clutter your bedroom. Take frequent breaks.

Day 10

Perform acts of random kindness. Pick 2 or three people in need and help them.

Day 11

Clock out of work on time. Have frequent breaks. Take a relaxing walk. Remember that all your meals should be lagom—not too little, not too much, just right.

Day 12

De-clutter your basement/attic.

Day 13

Prepare a lagom meal and share it with your neighbor.

Day 14

De-clutter your garage.

Day 15

Spend the day relaxing if it is a weekend. If it is a Friday then get your favorite video and watch it with your favorite drink in hand tonight.

This day should be a treat for yourself.

Have your favorite meal and enjoy your new uncluttered home. Walk around the house if you want to bask in this new experience.

After watching the show mull over your lagom experience, and decide if this is a good lifestyle for you.

CONCLUSION

I'd like to thank you and congratulate you for transiting my lines from start to finish.

I hope this book was able to help you to try the lagom experience for yourself.

If you tried the 15-day lagom challenge then you have had a taste of the Swedish minimalist lifestyle. The next step is to decide if this kind of lifestyle is a good fit for you. That decision I leave to you entirely.

I wish you the best of luck!

Printed in Great Britain
by Amazon

81443212R00038